Letter
From Egypt

Moira Andrew

illustrated by Alenka Trotovšek

Letter From Egypt

This is a work of fiction.

Printed in the United States of America

A 2 Z Press LLC

PO Box 582

Deleon Springs, FL 32130

bestlittleonlinebookstore.com

sizemore3630@aol.com

440-241-3126

ISBN: 978-1-954191-83-9

Dedication

For Erin, Genevieve, Joe, Sam, & Harry

Dear Miriam,
Just a line

to let you know
how things
are with us
and, of course to

thank you
(and your good man)
for all you did for us

at your busiest
time too, what, with
the census
and all.

I was quite exhausted
and the Baby was
beginning to make
Himself felt.

If it hadn't been
for all your help
that night
my Baby might
have died.

Good of you
to put up with
all our visitors...

...who'd have thought, six scruffy shepherds up and leaving their sheep like that?

...and didn't they ever smell? Still they were good-hearted and they meant well. I hope they brought some extra trade to the inn.

They looked in need
of a hot drink
and a meal.

And what about those kings, Miriam? Kneeling there in their rich robes and all? And me in nothing but my old blue dress!

Joseph said not to worry, it was Jesus they'd come to see. Real gentlemen they were. But what funny things to give a Baby — gold and myrrh and frankincense.

That's men all over!
It wouldn't cross
their minds to
bring a shawl!

We had to take
the long way home
and I'm so tired
of looking at sand!

Joseph has picked up
a few jobs mending
this and that so we're
managing quite well.
Jesus grows bonnier
every day and thrives
on this way of life,

The End

Moira Andrew is a travelling poet and children's author who was born and educated in Scotland. She has worked in most areas of primary education as a teacher, head teacher, and college lecturer.

Moira taught creative writing part-time at the University of Glamorgan. She has written seven books on the creative arts for teachers, (Belair). She also writes stories and poems for children, *Wish a Wish*, (Poetry Space), is the most recent. She has tens of poetry collections for adults in publication, *Geese and Daughters* (IDP) and *Imagine a Kiss*, (Dempsey & Windle) are her most recent. Moira also has a very special book, *Looking through Water*, (Poetry Space) - *a sensitive and thoughtful* collection of poetry documenting her failing sight that is being recorded by the RNIB as a Talking Book for the blind.

Moira has over 100 titles and
more than 2500 poems to her credit!

Some Other Books
by Moira Andrew

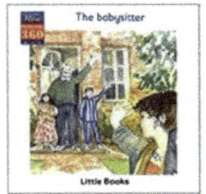     

 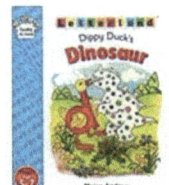 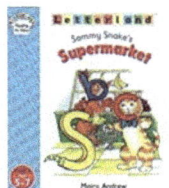  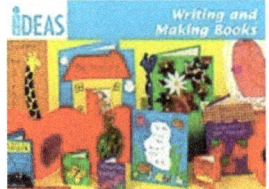

And many, many more to come!

In 1989 Moira Andrew, then the head of a primary school in Bristol, UK, was sorting the mail. She found a flyer from a new publisher called Belair. She found it very interesting; all the subjects covered except for Creative Writing, Poetry, and Art!

A few weeks later, the first of her books "Language in Colour" was contracted! In the 1990's-2000's, these books for teachers were in every school in the UK. Moira became a full time writer. Many teachers that she knows still have their personal copies.

Unfortunately, they are long out of print as the curriculum has changed. It became much more prescriptive, and creativity discouraged! What a waste! (Though you can still find copies if you go on line.)

Moira wrote most weeks for the teachers' magazine, 'Child Education' (Scholastic) and often her poetry appeared as Posters for the classroom wall. Here are the covers of the complete set. They are brim full of creative ideas, lesson plans, children's work, and suggestions for display. Still writing every day, she has 101 books to her name and there are currently 5 more being published! Moira is a remarkable woman!

Samples of Moira's Lovely Poster Poems

(Scholastic)

Dragon Feast

If you want to feed a dragon,
start with something hot,
spicy prawns in Vindaloo,
the fiercest that you've got.

They like all kinds of fiery food,
red-hot chillies, pickled limes,
sausages in mustard, peppered crab
with toast burned fourteen times.

Follow this with deep-fried mango
in a flaming brandy sauce,
and some of the very strongest mints
to finish with, of course.

Moira Andrew

My Little Sister

They said they'd let me
hold her in the garden
for a photograph.

'Be careful,' they said.
'She's new and tiny
and very very precious.'

They sat me on a chair,
my legs dangling.
'Ready now?' they asked.

And they placed her
on my lap, wriggling and wet.
'Smile,' they said.

I tried, but it wasn't easy
to hold the baby and smile,
both at the same time.

Moira Andrew

Fire

Fire lives in the heart
of a summer poppy,
spills blood-red
from the rising sun.

Fire winks its eye
from the geranium,
dreams of flame
all the long afternoon.

Fire sleeps in the
dark of a night rose,
slumbers ash-cold
in the pale moonlight.

Moira Andrew

Visit Moira's Website

Visit www.moiraandrew.com for
all the latest titles and
more information about Moira!

www.ingramcontent.com/pod-product-compliance
Lightning Source LLC
Chambersburg PA
CBHW041523120626

46551CB00018B/2551